# Suburbia
## & other sign posts pointing west

Debby Johnson

Suburbia and other signposts pointing west

Copyright © 2013 Debby Johnson. LoveBlind Publishing.
(www.loveblindmusic.com)

All rights reserved.

ISBN-13: **978-0615888514**
ISBN-10:0615888518

# DEDICATION

This is for those who have inspired, encouraged and stood by me while I was distracted and forgot to do laundry, failed to cook dinner and generally put up with my single-minded compulsion to get this book written. It's for those who have put up with the crazy person that I was. (Okay that I am.)

In all seriousness, this is for my amazing, wonderful, completely supportive husband, Ron. You are the light of my life, the love I searched way too long to find and the most fabulous man a girl could ask for. You put up with me, no matter what crazy scheme I come up with.

And to my children, Sarah, Courtney, Melissa, Jeremy and Christopher…each of you are more than I could have ever asked for.

Suburbia and other signposts pointing west

**Suburbia**

Grieve not for me
But where I began,
a refugee of life.
Middle-class
a voiceless,
nameless,
faceless mannequin.

Suits and ties
and blackberries
overload me,
weigh me down.
When all I really need
is the ocean's tongue
lashing my cheeks,
scratching, gnawing
my unblemished skin
kissing me
with the sting of salt
and sand
and air.

What I really need
is to live.
Unfettered.
Unrestrained.
Without judgment,
without regrets
Beliefs unquestioned.
Uncompromised.

**Someone**

Someone.
I used to know.
A sideways glance,
a reflection from the past,
fluttering hands,
squeaking sand,
a lilting laugh,
that shattered glass.

Someone.
I used to know.
Disappeared. Unrevered.
No longer here.
Just someone.
A sliver. A speck.
The whisper of a soul.
Contagious. Outrageous.
Dangerous.
Simplicity unfurled.
Insinuation.
Destinations.

Promises sighed -
carried like a threat
through the air.
Drifting. Fleeing.
Unspoken.
Needing.
Promises...unfulfilled.

A battle of wills,
alcohol and pills.
All from a glance,
some random chance.
Someone.
I used to know.

A heart turned to stone
never missed,
never mourned.

One last beat.
One last thunk,
stilled heart.
Useless junk.
Sins scattered
like moans
upon a spring breeze.
a corpse - empty skin.
Spirits adrift on the wind.

Someone.
I used to know.

**The List**

I hate The List.

Looking for a job,
or an adulterous kiss.
A quick stab,
feeling sad,
twisting the knife,
it ain't right.
We're all crazy
some more than most,
there's no denying
It's the host.

Secret meetings
in plain sight.
Everything happens
right online,
a virtual reality
in real time.

Freaks and geeks
John and Mary Jane,
Everything's together
Everyone's insane.

It's all about
pandering to dreams,
without even knowing
what that means.
The stab of a knife
and then a twist.
It's all about
what you missed.

It's no wonder,
no surprise -
List I hate you,
so full of lies.

## Fireflies in a Jar

Catch a shooting star
like fireflies in a jar,
Need them...feed them,
to make you who you are.

Crescendos crashing coast to coast,
Spam for dinner with buttered toast.
I hear the timbre shattering down traveling frantically from town to town.

I need them...I feed them...

The rhythmic sound of tires flop...flop..
slapping the asphalt road until we stop,
rolling in to another city, another dive,
sucking in the stench, proving we're still alive.

Raindrops splattering down in a staccato storm,
ten lonely people waiting for us to perform.

I feed them.. I need them...

Dreams that taunt and tantalize
becoming nothing but empty lies,
shattered promises lying just out of reach,
life laughing as its lessons teach.

I need them...I feed them...

How can I lament the sound of lullabies
that offers promise and then cries not yet...not yet, its not your time,
keep stretching moving, catch the next dime?

I feed them...I need them...

American Idol dreams
Listening for the fans screams
Peppered with today's realities,
hearing only hollow echoes shouting back at me.

Catch a shooting star
like fireflies in a jar,
Need them...feed them,
to find out who you are.

**Listen**

Listen...do you hear that sound?
It's my heart breaking
as it shatters
and hits the ground.

Don't hurt me more darling
don't make me sad and blue
Don't make my heart shatter
and break in two.

Love ain't the reason
I've heard it all before
Love ain't the reason
As you go back for more.

I wanna beg
I wanna plead
I wanna be
the one you need

Love ain't the reason
I've heard it all before
Love ain't the reason
As you go back for more.

Looking in the mirror
is an awful deed
Oh my darling
Why can't I be the one you need?

Love ain't the reason
I've heard it all before
Love ain't the reason
As you go back for more.

All I want is love
All I want is you
All I want is love
A heart that is true.

Love ain't the reason
I've heard it all before
Love ain't the reason
As you go back for more.

**Rolling Around In My Head**

The words roll around in my head,
Seductively teasing me in my bed
Like a guy in skin tight blue jeans
Well-toned abs and a hidden disease.
What are you supposed to do?
When the words are seducing you?
Soft and low they moan to me
Sometimes I just wish they'd let me be.
Loud and strong they yell all night
Come on, get up you wanna fight?

Leave me alone, let me be
Why are you always taunting me?

Flickering lights paint the street
Where all the pimps and hookers meet.
The words roll around in my head
Seductively teasing me in my bed.
I beg so loud, I beg so long
Pleading now, I know its wrong.
Dark and lonely its 2:00 a.m.
I have to finally pick up the pen.
Screaming silently I write my song
The words were dancing right along.
Maybe now they'll give me peace
'Cause I finally let them rise and speak.

The words roll around in my bed
Seductively teasing me in my head.

**Sub.Urbia**

Suburbia.
Mini vans and SUVs
Barbie moms and
silent pleas.
Sub. Urbia.

Mortgages,
out of hand
soccer dads,
empty homes,
everyone feels alone.
Suburbia.

Tattoos out of place,
long commutes
and a tired face,
Inland Empire to LA.
Suburb.I.A.

## The Dance


And we dance the dance
we always dance
humming the same stale old tune,
moving at odds but dancing again
Under the half moon.

Over and over
we practice our steps
swaying to the rusty bassoon.
Over and over
we dance the dance
by the light of distant moon.

When at long last
the music is done
We each return to our room.
All the long while
humming the same old tune.

**Voices in My Head**


I hear voices in my head
That's what the old lady said
Demons yell and demons shout
Let us in or let us out.

Tiny ants climb the walls,
Crawl the stairs and up the stalls
Bees buzz and fly about
While demons yell and demons shout.

Flowers bloom in the garden
All the while concrete hardens
Winds blast an evil moan
Talking to demons as they roam.

I hear voices in my head
That is what the child said
As she turned and looked at me
Make them go, please set them free.

## Just to touch the heavens

As the road gets dimmer
And I fight to see,
The darkness over takes me
And I fight just to be…

Just to feel the wind,
Just to hear the surf,
Just to touch the heavens,
Right here on earth.

Weariness is dragging on me
Trying to take me down
I'm so tired of being lonely,
Alone in a crowd.

Just to feel the wind,
Just to hear the surf,
Just to touch the heavens
Right here on earth.

I can hear the voices
As they play in my head
I can hear them whispering
As I lay down in bed.

Minivans and picket fences
Suburbia seems insane
Shopping trips and the dentist
Everything's always the same.

And all I want…all I want…
Just to feel the wind,
Just to hear the surf,
Just to touch the heavens,
Right here on earth.

Time drags on forever
Until I feel your touch,
Life is so much better
Its what means so much.

Trapped in your arms
I'm finally at peace
There'll be no harm
And I can be at ease.

My memories falter,
Of summers at the beach.
Where I can taste the salt air
And love is within reach.

Just to feel the wind,
Just to hear the surf,
Just to touch the heavens,
Right here on earth.

## In the Twilight of Our Slumber

You whispered in the twilight of our slumber
How each day, each step, had its number
And while no man may know his time,
Certainly each day we are dying.

And I tried, oh how I tried,
I couldn't help it, how I cried,
I couldn't imagine a day without you
If it were 100 years it'd be too soon.

And in the midst of my tears
I was faced with all my fears.
Nothing without you would be the same
There'd be no sunshine - only rain.

And when the tears had subsided
That's when I had decided
I'd make a list of things to do
And each one was with you.

In the twilight of our slumber
All that I could remember
Was the happiness you'd given me
So I whispered my silent plea.

Let our eternity begin right here,
While I can hold you close and near.
When its time for our December
Our love would stay a burning ember.

At last when we're done,
Too tired to carry on
We'd have one last cosmic kiss –
An eternity of peace and bliss.

The Heavens would shoot out stars
As again I held you in my arms.
My wish in the twilight of our slumber,
Was for our love to last forever.

Until the end of time, I want you to still be mine.

**Where has He Gone?**

Where has God gone?
When you cannot see Him
In the mountains majesty
Nor hear His voice
In the ocean's thunderous surf.

Has He abandoned you
Like some unwanted kitten by the roadside?
Or is He sleeping deep within your heart?
Celestial snores yet faint reminders
Of His infinite deeds done here on earth.

Where has He gone
when you don't need Him?
Some cosmic vacation to ski among the stars?
Where has He gone when you've forgotten
in the blink of an eye
diverted by neon lights of greed and lust?

Deep drink the breath of the icy air
And feel His love as it cuts into your lungs.
Cry out in pain for His loving hand
To hold you once again.

Where have you gone,
the voice implores
To the gentle love
that wraps around your soul.

Waiting for you...
as always,
He was here.

# Imposter

I am a fraud,
An imposter,
A 'never has been'
Clad in the clothes
of manufactured success,
Pulling tightly to my soul
the fabricated suits
of well-woven silk
lest peering eyes spot the gaping holes
eaten out by the dirty, creatures
that populate my garden at night.

I cling desperately to the accolades
thrown so carelessly and randomly,
scattered like rice at a wedding,
to fall where it may,
caring not
that the birds will eat it
and explode.

I am a fraud,
An imposter,
Riding on the crest of the wave,
heart pounding
loudly.

And the universe screams
in my ears.

Fraud.
Imposter.

## Pot Roast

I was cooking dinner
when the words slowly formed,
until they danced like an egg
in a pot of boiling water.

Solid…more real…
pecking at my brain,
what,
I wondered
did this have to do
with pot roast?

If I keep peeling potatoes
will they go away?
My feet shifting back and forth
to their rhythmic song.

Shall I carve the words on a carrot?
Can I scrawl them on a napkin?
Must I etch them in my brain?
The knife slips and a drop of blood
drips slowly down the drain.

I was cooking dinner.

And listening to the rain.

**Marbles**

The marbles clatter in my brain
Another thought I've misplaced again,
Replaced with gray strands
And aches and pains.

To age with dignity,
Oh, what a myth.
Instead it's a long death kiss.


**Filled With Gloom**

Leaden hearts filled with gloom
Danced around the darkened room
Aunt Mary had died tonight
And in her passing extinguished light.


**Her Face**

Lines etched in a face,
sorrow gently erased.
Compassionate eyes
became her disguise,
the strength of her soul,
keeping her whole.

## I am like the clock

I am like the clock
that's winding down.
A minute lost
here
and there,
unnoticed
like a solitary strand
of gray hair.
Unwinding.
Slowing down.
Forgetful.
Unreliable.
Unpredictable.
Overlooked,
unappreciated.

Un-
   winding-
      ing.

Until I stop,
but even that's so slow
no one notices
for a day
or two.

And even then
no one knows
exactly what to do.
A face.
Some hands.
Some gray strands.

## Mediocrity

Illuminated by the flicker of false light
I work alone.
Again.
Fingers dancing across the keys like tiny dancers
Trapped in a strange flamenco dance,
Staccato sounds driving the tempo of the words
As I struggle with the chance of success.
Terrified, the words tumble in a jumbled mess before me.
Mediocrity taunts me –
Seductively inviting me to stumble lest anyone discover
That I am not what I appear to be
And that all of my previous accolades
Are only brightly painted papers
Flapping in the wind,
Colours running randomly at the first rain.
Mediocrity…

The word feels comfortable in my mouth
Rolling between my tongue and teeth as though it belongs there,
Smooth and hard like a marble, it begs to be repeated.
Teasing me,
Begging to be swallowed up and drip warmly down my throat.
Only to choke me while I sleep.
Mediocrity…

Safe and warm it invites me to lay my head upon its shoulder,
Nestling in its comforting arms.
My fingers slow as the words trip up each other
And the slow, rhythmic crescendo in my brain rises,
Percolating, at the point of boiling.
I hear the kettle calling to me that my tea should be ready
If only I come and pour the bubbling water into my cup.
But I have no kettle. I don't even like tea…
A sigh seeps out my tightly pursed lips
My mind releasing the final steam from my skull,
As my fingers tire from their dance,
Lying limply as if to say they are done.
Mediocrity has at last come to my rescue,  (cont.. on next page)

Offering me salvation,
Splashing a life vest before my drowning soul.
And the critics will clamor with excitement,
Hanging on each syllable and verb,
"This is your finest work," they'll say.

My soul dances with relief,
Obscured by mediocrity…



**Monday**


I wrap my brain around the possibilities of Monday.
The promise that the morning sun gives
As it streams through the thinness
of the blue morning.
Fragile and full of promise,
Fresh scrubbed
and brimming with potential
Just a finger's breadth out of reach.

**The Beach**

This is not the beach of my youth.
I begged to return here only to walk upon its littered shores,
Where once warm sand had oozed between my toes
Now broken shards of shells slice them,
And I leave a vermilion trail in my wake.
Breathing in the memories of
Salt-water air tinged with the ocean's promise
Instead, I gasp for breath suffocating on my own dreams.

Limping past abandoned broken chairs
Gazing longingly into the dunes abloom with tiny yellow flowers
The thought of racing to them is drowned out by the
Pounding of my heart as it struggles to keep going.
Seagulls fly so gracefully, swooping gently
Until at last they see their prey down below
Diving fast to catch the strands
Of fine blonde hair blowing in the wind.

Aching head. Tired feet. Worn heart.
This is not the future of my youth.
Where do dreams go when they pass us by?
Do they linger on the distant horizon
Just long enough to whisper on the wind
Come and find us. We will wait here for you.
Marathon runs finally draw us near
Only to hear the screeching as the winds howl past us.
The dreams are not dead. They have forsaken us
For another golden tanned promise
On the beach of their youth.

## The Winter of My Days

Do you feel the icy fingers of despair
As they caress your long flowing hair?
Blonde strands weeping in the wind,
Screaming with an unheard voice
Never to be uttered again.

Do you feel the frigid claws of doom
As they stroke your shoulders
And call you to your room?

Does the chill seek warmth in your heart?
Or does it dampen the fires
For the long, never ending night?

Compassion camps outside the door
Come here never more.
Leave me lest I cry more tears
Let me wallow in my fears.

## Road to Chicago

I know the road to Chicago wasn't smooth,
Even the radio wouldn't stay in tune.
The roads were icy and so were you,
Maybe I said the words too soon.

I wanted to say I love you,
I wanted to make it last,
I needed to feel your love,
But perhaps I'm moving too fast.

Sometimes when the storms roll in,
You think about the way things have been.
Sun shining down on through the autumn leaves
Holding hands and sharing house keys.

I wanted to say I love you,
I wanted to make it last,
I needed to feel your love
But perhaps I'm moving too fast.

In the misty rain it seems so clear
I'm missing you and you're right here
I can tell that you're moving on
Wish I knew what I did wrong.

I wanted to say I love you,
I wanted to make it last,
I needed to feel your love,
But perhaps I'm moving too fast.

Wanting, needing it to be alright
Like make love in the middle of the night
Don't say the words that I can hear
Not while I still feel your warm so near.

I wanted to say I love you,
I wanted to make it last,
I needed to feel your love,

But perhaps I'm moving too fast.

## Find My Way

I lay alone in my single bed
All the dreams rolling in my head,
I'd come to LA to find my way
But now I just wait tables all day.
The whine of a motorcycle rolls by
Just like my hopes driving off to die

I'd come to LA to find my way
How can I make my dreams stay?
What am I going tell the folks back home
It rings…but I don't answer the phone.

I gotta find my way…I'm gonna find my way
I landed here to stay, not to fade away
Like the dreams rolling in my head
They're the stuff upon which I'm fed.

LA's a tough town they say
And I don't wanna let my dreams fade away
I can't let go – no matter what they said
All the dreams keep rolling through my head.

I gotta find my way…I'm gonna find my way
I landed here to stay, not to fade away
Like the dreams rolling in my head
They're the stuff upon which I'm fed.

You'll know my name, one day I'm sure
The city's used its wiles to lure
My dreams and hitching them to a star
It may take forever to get that far.
But that's ok, it's alright with me
One day you'll know me, you'll see.

I gotta find my way…I'm gonna find my way
I landed here to stay, not to fade away
Like the dreams rolling in my head
They're the stuff upon which I'm fed.

**Ringo's Song**

I wish I could make it better
I wish I could take it away
I wish I could make it better
So that you could stay.

You're not the same
As you used to be,
I can feel it now
Everyone one can see.

Its painful watching you
As you drift away
It's hard to smile and pretend
'Cause you'll be gone one day.

My heart is breaking
I wanna say its not so
If only there were something…
I don't want you to go

I wish I could make it better
I wish I could take it away
I wish I could make it better
So that you could stay.

I'll shed so many tears
The day that you leave me
For now I'm being brave
That's the person I'm going to be.

You're not the same,
I see it in your eyes
Your spirit is the same
Just hiding in this new disguise.

I wish I could make it better
I wish I could take it away
I wish I could make it better
So that you could stay.

No words can say
The feeling in my heart
I dread that final day
When we finally part.

I love you…
I love you so,
In every way
That, I hope you know.

I wish I could make it better
I wish I could take it away
I wish I could make it better
I really wish that you could stay.

*(Ringo was our dear sweet puppy. We miss you each and every day.)*

**Everywhere You Look**

It was the old girl friend, the girl next door,
There was even a half-eaten apple core.
Everywhere you look, everything you see,
Oh, how I wish that it could be me.

I wanna be your muse, your inspiration
I wanna be one of your creations.
I wanna be the one you hold so tight
Then I know everything's alright.

A shining star, the special light
That inspires you in the night,
The very air you breathe,
Let me be the one that you need.

I wanna be your muse, your inspiration
I wanna be one of your creations.
I wanna be the one you hold so tight
Then I know everything's alright.

You are the pilot guiding my dreams
And when we're together it always seems
Like gliding through the heavens and the stars
Together we can go so very far.

I wanna be your muse, your inspiration
I wanna be one of your creations.
I wanna be the one you hold so tight
Then I know everything's alright.

Everywhere you look, everything you see,
Oh, how I wish that you could see me.

## Grand Central Station

Still a million miles away from my dreams
and nothing is ever quite what it seems,
It's like running in circles, faster on the wheel
always wishing- wishing for that magical deal.

You've just gotta believe -
believe that it's real
hoping and working
Imagine how it'll feel.

Yeah baby, I can tell
its really on the way.
The universe is shifting
I'm gonna have my say.

And when I do,
babe watch out,
you won't have to listen
to hear this cosmic shout.

I want it
I need it
I dream it
I bleed it.

One day baby
we'll be singing out loud
feet on the ground
head in the clouds.

Do you want it
living the dream with me?
You want babe -
Just try it and see.

It's a one way ticket to paradise.
Its adulation.
Inspiration.
Grand Central Station.

It's a shooting the star
the whole world can see.
Let's do it together -
just you and me.

A melody
sweet and strong,
something to live
when we're both gone.

I don't want to fade away,
take me through the haze
take me, take me -
right to center stage.

Inspiration.
Adulation.
Let's ride the train
to Grand Central Station.

Dare to dream -
dare to believe,
nothing is ever
quite as it seems.

Are you ready?
I know you are.
Come with me
be my shooting star.

Adulation.
Inspiration.
A one way ticket
to Grand Central Station.

## The Button

The button lay there
on the bathroom counter.
A week.
Two weeks.
Finally it had been there
so long I lost count.

I waited to see who
would pick it up first,
or so I said,
when really there
was comfort with
the careless disarray
of my life.

Simple,
Round.
White.
Unobtrusive.
Unmemorable.
It had become a fixture
Seemingly right where it belonged.

My button spoke to me.
I heard it
but I did not listen.

**I'm Torn...**

I'm torn apart I wanna stay
For another minute or another day
But in the end it's all the same
Gotta just run and face the pain

The world is calling out my name
Stayin' here just ain't the same
I got a hole where my heart should be
I gotta climb that mountain or sail the sea

The howlin' wind screams my name
Staying here just ain't the same.
I guess the only way to quiet my soul
Means leaving your heart with an empty hole


**Same Ole Song**

Every day you run and play
The sky is blue but the clouds are grey
cracker jacks and marshmallow pies
Nothing's changed but the look in your eyes

Time rolls on, drums stay strong
Passing years don't seem so long
Nothing new, nothing wrong
Same ole tune, different song.

## The Passion of My Youth

I miss the passion...
the passion of my youth.
Or is it the youth of my passion?
I'm not certain.
The passion,
that passion which once sprang forth
with such vigor
that shot out,
heaven bound.
Now, it churns and boils
rolling beneath the surface
like seismic waves
moving things blind to it.
Reaching out,
touching,
exerting its wrath
all the same.

Middle aged,
seasoned,
scorched by the fires of life,
though they need not erupt
on every occasion.
Yes,
I miss the youth
of my passion...
yet as its twilight looms,
dangling overhead,
I know its greatest force
is yet to be heard.

**Home**
I'd come home to bury my toes in the soft white sands of the Gulf Coast,
To walk upon the dunes and breathe deeply of the salty air
Savoring it as it stung my lungs, begging them to expand just a little more.

I'd come home…

Home to a place I didn't know and people I didn't recognize.
Home to a place that no longer held any appeal to me or I to it,
Where the soft southern drawl twanged against my eardrums
Leaving it ragged from listening so long to a language I couldn't understand.

I'd come home…

Home to a place where I wasn't born and held no bondage over me.
Home to a place that was as foreign to me as the shores of Normandy,
Where the only thing I recognized was the lapping of the waves
As they tried desperately to unbury that which was buried deep.

I'd come home…

Home to bury the ache in my soul and dull the gut-wrenching pain
That consumed me from the inside out with guilt-riddled memories
Of a life I used to know but whose details had long been forgotten,
Like the tattoos of a sailor, which spoke of ports and women he had visited.

I'd come home…

Home. A place where I didn't belong and yet it seemed the only place that I could be.
A place where the smell of grits and hush puppies wafted out of open doors
Just as readily as fresh cut grass on a Saturday morning, calling out to children
As they played hopscotch on the sidewalk with crisp freshly chalked lines.

I'd come home…

I'd come home to bury my sins in the soft warm white sands of the gulf.
Returning to have the crystal blue waters of the ocean lap up my soul,
So that I could at long last find peace and solace in the bright sunshine.
I was finally home.

## Mortality

The bugler's cry is rung.
Mortality charges in.

I faced the day with hazy eyes
cloudy and drawn unable to see
anything left but the days
that scatter and fly
like brittle autumn leaves
soaring on the wind.
Fast. Furious. Out of control.
At the mercy of the wind.

I no longer darken the door.
Will anyone notice
that I knock no more?
Will my scent linger in the room?
A pungent perfume that fades away.
Disappearing. Gone.
Would any of it matter?
What have I done?
What will I do?
Nothing. There's no more time.
Silence creeps into place,
stealing away the bugler's face.
Mortality sneaks in.

Once dreams stretched before me,
now they're merely lines etched on my face.
Mortality is calling.
I've got to take my place.
But I don't want to go.
there's so much I want to know.
But mostly - I want to matter.
Tears fall as I watch
the leaves scatter.

I am just a whisper in the wind,
A story of places I've never been.
Dandelions floating in the air.
Confusion and sadness everywhere.
Settling in to my skin.

Blemishes full of sin.
Dandelions in an empty field.
Dreams escaping. Unfulfilled.
I am just...
a whisper in the wind.

**Snickers**

Snickers was a valiant dog
Bonnie brave and true
When I'd whistle for the boys
He'd come running too.

Snickers was a valiant dog
Bonnie brave and true
He'd curl up on my feet at night
And stay the whole night through.

Snickers was a valiant dog
Bonnie brave and true
He'd run and fetch and shake
And even howl upon cue.

Snickers was a valiant dog
Bonnie brave and true
He kept me safe from strangers
There was nothing he wouldn't do.

Snickers was a valiant dog
Bonnie brave and true
He rescued me from the burning fire
And that's all I can tell you.

Snickers was a valiant dog
Bonnie brave and true
He kept me safe right to the end
That's what Snickers did do.

## Meet the Author

*Wife. Mother. Karate Instructor.*

These are just a few of the labels that you could hang around my neck. In addition, I also co-own a successful graphic design & web design business with my husband. Oh yeah, and I'm an artist, photographer and dreamer.

My wish is to leave this world a better place than I found it, to make a difference, touching a life or two. I hate bullies. I love the colour pink. I hate ice cream and adore anchovies. I am passionate about my family. I am what I appear to be. I believe anything is possible.

My work has been published in various regional publications. I've also been a contributor to the book, *Cookie: A Love Story by Brett Sembler.* Currently I'm working on a children's book, a novel and a mystery. Did I mention that I'm a chronic multi-tasker?

If you'd like to reach me, feel free. My email address is debby@debbyjohnson.com. I'd love to hear from you.

*Words are merely illusions upon which to hang our hats.*

www.ingramcontent.com/pod-product-compliance
Lightning Source LLC
Chambersburg PA
CBHW070753050426
42449CB00010B/2454